Retold by Kathryn Smith
Illustrated by Stuart Trotter
Religious consultant: Meryl Doney
Language consultant: Betty Root

This is a Parragon Publishing book
First published in 2004

Parragon Publishing
Queen Street House
4 Queen Street
BATH BA1 1HE, UK

Printed in Indonesia

STORIES FROM THE BIBLE

Jonah
and
the
Whale

_p_

Jonah was a quiet man who liked
living a quiet life. But God had a job
for Jonah. It was a very important job.

"Go and tell the wicked people of Nineveh to change their ways," God told him. "Teach them to be good, and to follow my laws."

But Jonah didn't want to go.

"Those bad people don't deserve God's love!" he thought. "They deserve to be punished. I won't go."

Jonah decided to run away and hide from God. So he jumped on a boat—a boat sailing to a land far away from Nineveh.

"Wake me when we arrive," Jonah told the captain as he paid his fare. Then he went below deck and hid in the dark.

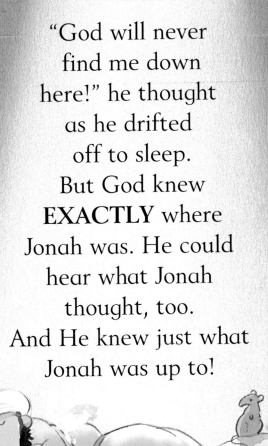

"God will never
find me down
here!" he thought
as he drifted
off to sleep.
But God knew
EXACTLY where
Jonah was. He could
hear what Jonah
thought, too.
And He knew just what
Jonah was up to!

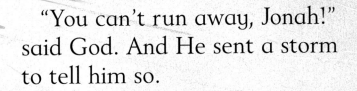

"You can't run away, Jonah!"
said God. And He sent a storm
to tell him so.

WHOOSH! went the wind.
SWOOSH! went the waves.

"HELP!" cried the sailors
as the boat tossed on the sea.
But Jonah stayed fast asleep.

The storm grew angrier and angrier.

"HELP *!*" cried the sailors. "Row for the shore!"

But the waves were too tall. **WHOOSH! SWOOSH!** They crashed onto the deck and washed the oars out to sea.

"Throw the cargo overboard," shouted the captain. HEAVE HO! SPLASH! But it made no difference. The boat was sinking.

"Wake up, Jonah," yelled the sailors. "Pray for your life!"

"The gods are angry!" shouted the captain.
"Someone on board has upset them!"
Everybody looked at each other. Who could it be?

"Not me!" cried
the cabin boy.

"Not me!" cried the cook.

"Not us!" cried the sailors.

"It must be somebody!" said
the captain. "We'll draw lots
to find out who."

"Wait!" shouted Jonah. "It's me!
My God is the one true God. He sent
the storm, because I disobeyed him."

The sailors rolled their eyes and shook their heads. "Now what do we do?" they howled. "We're all going to drown."

"God isn't angry with you," said Jonah. "If you throw me overboard, the storm will stop."

"We can't do that!" they cried. "You'll drown!"

But Jonah was brave. "Do as I say," he said.

HEAVE HO! SPLASH! The sailors tossed Jonah into the stormy sea. The storm stopped at once.

Jonah slowly sank to the very bottom of the sea.

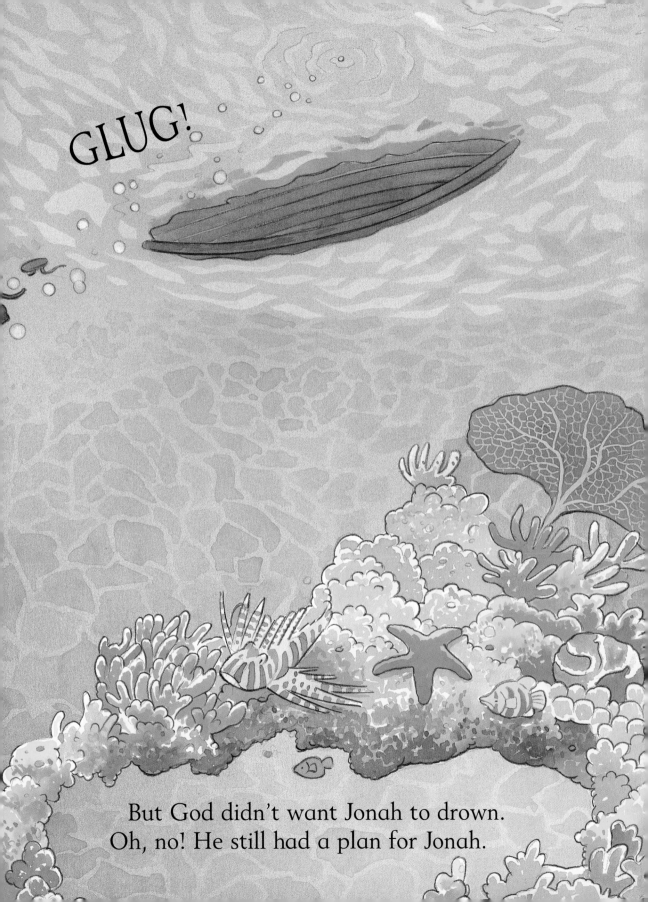

GLUG!

But God didn't want Jonah to drown.
Oh, no! He still had a plan for Jonah.

"Open your eyes, Jonah," said God. "I'm going to save you."

Jonah opened his eyes, just in time to see the biggest whale he had ever seen.

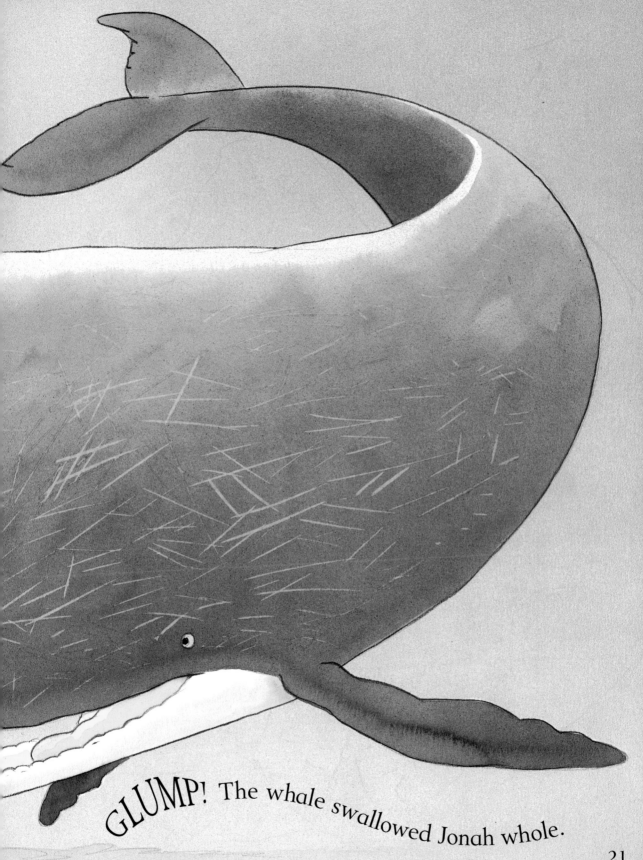

GLUMP! The whale swallowed Jonah whole.

Down, down, down slid Jonah, into the whale's belly. PLOP ! He landed on a bed of seaweed.

It was dark inside. It was cold inside. But Jonah wasn't afraid. He knew now that God could see and hear him, wherever he was. Even in the deep, dark belly of a whale!

So Jonah prayed. He prayed as hard as he could.

"I'm right here, God," he cried. "Thank you for saving my life. I'm ready to do as you ask."

Of course, God already knew where Jonah
was. He could hear Jonah's prayers, too.
And He knew just what was in his heart!
So God sent the whale to shore.

"HICCUP!" went the whale.

Out of the whale's mouth flew Jonah.
He sailed through the air and landed
with a thud on the beach.

Then God
spoke to Jonah.
"Get ready, Jonah,"
He said. "Get ready
to go to Nineveh!"
And this time Jonah
obeyed. He hurried there
as fast as his legs would
carry him.

What did Jonah tell the people of Nineveh?
He told them what he had learned, of course.

"Listen to me," he cried. "God sees everything
we do. He hears everything we say. And He
knows exactly what is in our hearts. If you are
truly sorry and change your wicked ways, He
will forgive you."

What did the people of Nineveh do?
They listened, of course.

"We're sorry, God," they prayed. "We will change. Forgive us!" And God forgave them, just as He had forgiven Jonah.